KT-132-280

NB 1841 384739 8006

Leabharlanna Atha Cliath
CABRA LIBRARY
Invoice : 03/3074 Price EUR17.32
Title: Verdi
Class: 780·92 VER

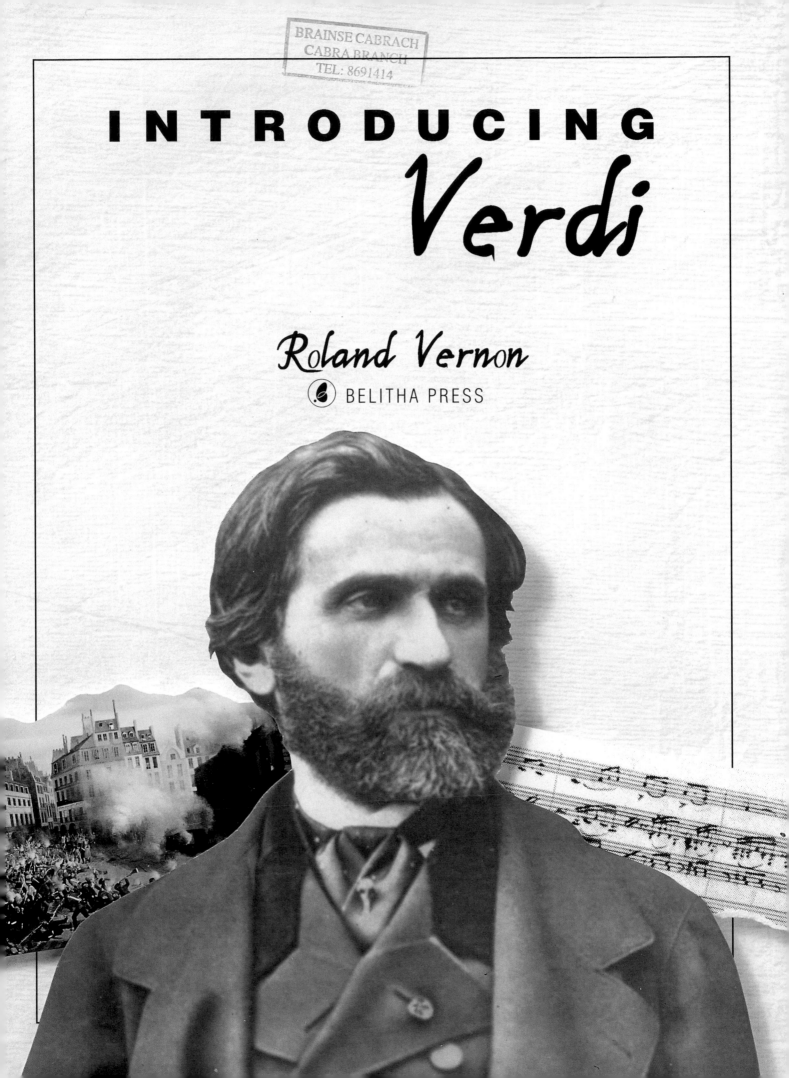

BRAINSE CABRACH
CABRA BRANCH
TEL: 8691414

INTRODUCING
Verdi

Roland Vernon

BELITHA PRESS

This edition published in 2002 by
Belitha Press
A member of Chrysalis Books plc
64 Brewery Road, London N7 9NT

Copyright © in this format Belitha Press
Text copyright © Roland Vernon
Illustration copyright © Ian Andrew

Editors: Christine Hatt and Claire Edwards
Designer: Wilson Design Associates
Picture researcher: Juliet Duff

All rights reserved. No part of this book may be reproduced
or utilized in any form or by any means, electronic or mechanical,
including photocopying, recording or by any information storage
and retrieval system, without permission in writing from the publisher
except by a reviewer who may quote brief passages in a review.

Printed in Hong Kong

British Library Cataloguing in Publication Data
for this book is available from the British Library.

ISBN 184138 473 9

Picture acknowledgements:
AKG, London: back cover , title page, 8 Museo Teatrale alla
Scala, Milan, 12 left, 14 top Musée Carnavalet, Paris, 15 Gallerie
d'Arte Moderna, Florence, 18 bottom, 21 left, 23 top, 25 left, 26,
27 top. Property of Archivio Storico Ricordi – used by permission:
front cover, end papers, 10 bottom, 12 right, 27 centre. Bridgeman
Art Library: 23 bottom Private Collection, 28 Ricordi, Milan.
Donald Cooper/Photostage: 11 top, 17, 18 top, 25 right.
ET Archive: 7 bottom and 9 bottom Museo Teatrale alla Scala,
Milan, 9 top Museo Bibliografico Musicale Bologna, 11 bottom
Risorgimento Museum, Turin, 16, 20 Palazzo Pubblico Siena,
21 right Museo Civico Modigliana. Mary Evans Picture Library:
14 bottom, 22 bottom, 24 both, 29 bottom. Ronald Grant
Archive: 19 top. Image Select: 13 bottom, 29 top. Istituto
Nazionale di Studi Verdiani: 7 top, 22 top. Moviestore Collection:
27 bottom. Museo Teatrale alla Scala, Milan: 6, 9 centre, 13 top.
Scala: Cover Casa di Riposo per artisti G. Verdi, Milan, 10 top
Museo Teatrale alla Scala, Milan. Villa Verdi, Sant' Agata,
Busseto: 19 bottom.

ONTENTS

MACBETH

MUSICA di G. VERDI.

MILANO
DALLO STABILIMENTO NAZIONALE
TIPO DI GIO. RICORDI

Introducing Verdi

Opera was hugely popular during the nineteenth century, especially in Italy. Of all Italy's opera composers, the greatest and most loved was Giuseppe Verdi. Verdi was a man of the theatre. He understood how music could be used to create powerful drama and he had a great gift for matching poetry to tunes. His career as a composer lasted 60 years. During this time he kept alive the glorious tradition of Italian opera single-handedly. Verdi was also a **patriot**, and his music encouraged fellow Italians to rebel against their foreign rulers. Although he became an important public figure and a national hero, he was also a very private person. He did not like interference, and was deaf to both praise and criticism. He stubbornly believed only in himself and his own music. This eventually won him the respect of the world.

THE INNKEEPER'S SON

The house where Verdi was born, in Le Roncole, has been turned into a museum in honour of the composer.

Carlo Verdi and his wife Luigia kept a small inn at Le Roncole, a village in the **Parma** district of Italy. They were also the village grocers, so had to work hard for a living. On 9 October 1813 they had a son, and called him Giuseppe. It was a dangerous time for north Italy. The French army was being driven out, and troops of different nationalities were advancing through the region, often burning everything in their path. Luigia once hid in the church bell-tower to protect her baby.

Giuseppe was a shy, intelligent boy, who showed a great interest in music. He was spellbound by the sound of the church organ, and loved to listen to travelling musicians who passed through Le Roncole. His parents encouraged him, and saved up to buy an old **spinet**, which he soon mastered. He was sent to school in the nearby town of Busseto, and given music lessons. At the age of ten, he was appointed organist at the church in Le Roncole.

All through Verdi's life, Italy was the scene of many wars, revolutions and uprisings. When he was a baby, his mother had to flee with him from nearby battles.

Antonio Barezzi was responsible for launching Verdi's career, providing the young man with opportunities and money. Verdi never forgot his kindness.

While at school in Busseto, Giuseppe met Antonio Barezzi, a wealthy merchant who managed a local **amateur** orchestra. Barezzi became like a second father to Giuseppe, and welcomed the young man into his household. Giuseppe was soon hard at work composing many pieces of music for Barezzi's orchestra to perform. By the time he had reached the age of 16, he had also fallen in love with the merchant's daughter, Margherita.

Northern Italy in 1813

At the time of Verdi's birth, Italy was not a single country as it is now, but was divided into a number of separate states. Some were ruled by noble families, some by the Roman Catholic Church, and others by foreign governments. During the eighteenth century, most of northern Italy had been ruled by the Austrian royal family, the Habsburgs. In 1734, the small **Duchy** of Parma, where Verdi was born and grew up, was given to a member of the Spanish royal family.

In 1796 the brilliant young French general Napoleon Bonaparte invaded and conquered most of Italy. After three years, the armies of Austria and Russia drove him out, but in 1800 Napoleon returned and was soon in control of northern Italy again. The French remained there until Napoleon fell from power in 1814. Then Austria claimed back northern Italy as part of the Habsburg empire. The Duchy of Parma was handed over to the Austrian emperor's daughter.

The town of Busseto, where the young Verdi became known as a local prodigy.

But the time had come for Giuseppe to leave Busseto and receive a proper musical training. In 1832, he travelled to Milan, the biggest city in northern Italy, and applied to join the famous music **conservatory** there. But to the surprise of all his friends and family at home, who were extremely proud of his talent, he failed the entrance examination. Giuseppe himself was deeply upset, but decided to stay in Milan anyway. He arranged to take music lessons privately, and Antonio Barezzi generously agreed to help him pay for his studies.

A PROMISING YOUNG COMPOSER

M ilan was an exciting, modern city and an important centre for music. Barezzi sent Giuseppe money and arranged for him to have his own seat at the city's magnificent opera house, La Scala. Giuseppe then began making a name for himself as a promising young composer and conductor.

In 1836 Giuseppe returned to Busseto to marry Margherita Barezzi, and to take up the job of town music director. Most of his time was spent teaching the piano and composing for the local orchestra. Meanwhile, his friends in Milan sent letters encouraging him to try composing an opera. Intrigued at the idea, he began to sketch out some scenes. But in August 1838, tragedy struck when his daughter Virginia died, aged only 17 months.

La Scala opera house, in Milan, was the heart of Italian music. It was an honour for the young Verdi to have his operas performed there.

BRAINSE CABRACH

The following year, Giuseppe went back to Milan with his family. His opera was complete and he wanted to find a theatre company willing to stage it. But soon after he arrived, his other child, Icilio, also died. Better news came at last, when the director of La Scala, Bartolomeo Merelli, agreed to put on the opera, which was called *Oberto*. The **première**, on 17 November 1839, was a great success, and immediately established Verdi as an important new composer of opera. Merelli was delighted, and **commissioned** three more works.

Gioacchino Rossini (1792–1868)

ITALIAN OPERA AT THE START OF VERDI'S CAREER

Early nineteenth-century Italian opera inherited many of its traditions from a former era. The most important was called *bel canto*, which literally means 'beautiful singing'. Singers were trained to show off their voices in fast runs of notes, high leaps and delicate twirls, all sung with ease and beauty. The leading *bel canto* composer of the early nineteenth century was Gioacchino Rossini, who wrote huge numbers of highly successful operas and retired at the age of 37. He had two successors – Gaetano Donizetti (1797–1848) and Vincenzo Bellini (1801–1835). Much of Verdi's early work was composed in the style of these three popular musicians.

There was a great demand for new operas in early nineteenth-century Italy, and composers wrote at high speed. Skilful singing was considered more important than either music or drama. Composers often used the same music for several operas, with completely different stories and words. As a result, tragic scenes were sometimes accompanied by jolly, lilting music, which to later generations seemed very inappropriate.

Verdi was full of confidence until the three family tragedies that nearly finished his career.

The next opera was a comedy called *Un Giorno di Regno* (King for a Day). But Verdi suffered another disaster, which put all ideas of comedy out of his mind. Margherita died on 18 June 1840. Lonely and miserable, Giuseppe went home to Busseto and thought seriously about giving up music for ever. *Un Giorno di Regno* was staged in August 1840, but was a total failure. The music was weak, the singing was poor, and the audience whistled impatiently throughout. This unhappy period hardened Giuseppe's feelings. He was never again interested in what other people said about his music, no matter whether they praised it or criticized it.

Margherita Barezzi, Verdi's first wife, who died too early to witness her husband's rise to fame and fortune.

A HERO FOR ITALY

 lthough Verdi was depressed, on a winter evening at the end of 1840 he was persuaded to read through a new **libretto**. It was about the Jewish people and their struggle for freedom from **Babylon**. Verdi reluctantly agreed to compose the new opera, called *Nabucco*, and was soon deeply involved in his work. Finally, on 9 March 1842, *Nabucco* was produced at La Scala opera house and it immediately turned Verdi into a national hero. One particular chorus, when the Jews sing lovingly about their homeland, was taken up by Italians everywhere as a patriotic anthem. Its beautiful melody expressed Italy's longing to be a united country, free from Austrian rule. Verdi had suddenly become a political figure, a leading **nationalist**.

The interior of La Scala opera house, built by Milan's Austrian rulers, became a place where revolutionary plots were whispered against them.

Verdi's handwritten manuscript for 'Va, pensiero', the chorus in *Nabucco* that remained a hit throughout the composer's life.

A modern production of *Nabucco* shows the cast singing the chorus that made Verdi's reputation (see below left).

Verdi's next opera, *I Lombardi*, was first performed in 1843, and was also praised as a great patriotic statement. It tells the story of brave **Crusaders** from Lombardy (the province around Milan) who fight to rescue the Holy Land from **Saracens**. After this came *Ernani*, another opera with a political message. It was based on a story by French **republican** writer Victor Hugo, whom the Austrian authorities considered politically dangerous. But they knew Verdi was so popular, there might be riots if they banned one of his operas.

In *Nabucco*, Verdi broke away from *bel canto* and traditional Italian opera. He used a larger orchestra and his music contained more force. The singing was less pretty and elaborate, but much more dramatic. It closely matched the feelings expressed in the words. The audience thought this was very exciting, but some critics said that Verdi was destroying the art of beautiful singing.

Every opera company in Italy, and many abroad, now wanted to stage Verdi's works. He was a good businessman, and did not hesitate to ask for enormous fees. Rossini had retired, Bellini was dead, and Donizetti, tragically, was about to lose his mind. Verdi became the only hope for the future of Italian opera. His melodies were played on **barrel organs** and sung by people as they walked along the streets.

THE RISORGIMENTO

Risorgimento, an Italian word meaning 'revival', was the name given to the political movement that aimed to free Italy and unite it as one country. The Risorgimento was very active in Milan, where secret societies met in cafés or opera houses to discuss politics. Groups such as the Carbonari were formed, which plotted revolution against Austria. The republican writer Giuseppe Mazzini (1805–1872) founded an organization called Young Italy, which he hoped would rouse ordinary people to rebel.

The Risorgimento also encouraged new literature and music. Verdi's operas of this period were strongly influenced by the political mood in Milan at the time. After the success of *Nabucco*, he was welcomed into a circle of high-society friends, who met to talk about exciting new ideas in art and politics. They were known as liberals, and one of the most outspoken was Countess Maffei (1814–1886). She became Verdi's friend for life, and her Milan home was an important meeting place for liberals who supported the Risorgimento.

Risorgimento leader Mazzini was imprisoned for plotting revolt.

THE GALLEY-SLAVE YEARS

It was very fashionable to wear a beard like Verdi's in mid-nineteenth-century Italy, as a way of showing support for the Risorgimento.

V erdi suffered a mysterious illness every time he started working hard on an opera. The worst pain was in his throat, but he had bad headaches and stomach cramps as well. The illness was almost certainly brought on by tension, and was a sign that he was overworking. In 1846 he was so ill, one newspaper actually reported that he had died. His doctors ordered him to rest for six months.

The title page of an early edition of *Macbeth*. The picture shows a scene when Macbeth (right) meets the witches.

Verdi called this busy period of his life 'the **galley**-slave years', because there was no time for anything except hard labour. As well as composing, he always tried to attend rehearsals, because he liked to make sure that his works were properly prepared by singers and orchestra. He was often frustrated if details were not quite perfect.

In 1847, Verdi produced his greatest work so far. It was *Macbeth*, based on the play by **Shakespeare**. Verdi appreciated good drama, and the brilliance of Shakespeare's play brought out his best qualities as a composer. His music fully expresses the fear, the horror and the tragedy of Shakespeare's original. Verdi worked hard with the lead singers, so that they would interpret their roles correctly. He wanted them to understand his new ideas about opera – that words and drama were more important than beautiful singing. *Macbeth*'s première, in Florence on 14 March 1847, was a wild success. There were 38 **curtain-calls**, and Verdi was escorted back to his hotel by a vast, cheering crowd.

Later the same year, Verdi visited Paris. He stayed there for many months and spent most of his time with Giuseppina Strepponi, a former opera star who now taught singing in the city. She had been a friend and supporter of Verdi during his early years in Milan.

Giuseppina Strepponi, painted when she was one of Italy's greatest opera singers. The music is Verdi's *Nabucco*.

Giuseppina took part in the first production of *Nabucco*, but retired soon after, her voice worn out by overwork. In 1847 she and Verdi became lovers, which they remained for the next 50 years.

In the nineteenth century, Paris was Europe's musical capital. The Paris Opéra (above) staged some of Verdi's greatest works.

The 1848 Revolution in Paris gave hope to other people in Europe whose rulers were harsh and unpopular.

$\mathcal{A}$ TIME OF REVOLUTIONS

$\mathcal{L}$ ouis-Philippe, the king of France, was forced to **abdicate** in February 1848, after the people of Paris rose up in revolution. Rebellions broke out in several other European cities that year, including Milan, where 1700 street barricades blocked the city. After this 'Five Days' revolt, Austrian troops pulled out of Milan. On hearing the news, Verdi rushed back from Paris to take part in the freedom celebrations. But his hopes were short-lived. By June it became clear that the city would fall to Austria again, and Verdi returned to Paris.

Rebels in southern Italy suffered an important defeat on 15 May 1848, and foreign rule was imposed once again.

BRAINSE CABRACH
CABRA BRANCH
TEL: 8691414

After the 1848 Revolution, life in Paris was chaotic. Meanwhile, parts of Italy were still up in arms, battling against their former rulers. To encourage them, Verdi wrote a battle-hymn called 'Sound the Trumpet', which he hoped might one day become the national anthem of a free Italy. This hope was never fulfilled.

Verdi's most important work at this time was an opera called *La Battaglia di Legnano*. It was about an eleventh-century battle, in which a German emperor was defeated by northern Italians. The opera was a great success at its première in Rome, in January 1849. Two weeks later, Rome was declared a free republic. Verdi's opera was perfect for the mood of the moment.

But by the summer of 1849, Italy's revolutions were collapsing. The most powerful Italian leader, Charles Albert, king of **Piedmont**, was finally defeated by Austria and forced into **exile**. Meanwhile, the republic of Rome fell to French troops. Italy's dream of freedom from foreign rule had come to a tragic end.

Verdi returned to Busseto. He was saddened by the failure of Italy's uprising, but found consolation in work. He began to sketch out new musical ideas, and to experiment with ways of making operas more powerful on stage. His galley-slave years were over. He was rich and famous enough to retire, if he wanted, and free to compose what he wanted, at his own pace.

The Battle of Legnano was fought on 29 May 1176. Nearly 700 years later, Verdi's opera of the same name had the audience enthusiastically waving patriotic banners and singing along in the choruses.

RIGOLETTO – A NEW STYLE

Verdi's music now became more adventurous. The first opera that showed his change of style was *Rigoletto*, completed in 1851. *Rigoletto's* original story was about a heartless king who betrays an innocent girl. But the **censors** thought this story might turn people against their royal rulers, so Verdi turned the king into a duke. When *Rigoletto* was performed, it became his greatest success yet. He was the most popular opera composer in Europe, and his dramatic style of vocal music became the fashion. All the great singers wanted to perform roles in Verdi operas.

This card, which is an advertisement, shows a dramatic scene from *Rigoletto*, and includes a portrait of Verdi.

Italian operas written before Verdi's time were divided into separate **arias**, **recitatives**, duets and other numbers, and this interrupted the smooth running of the drama. But Verdi wrote parts of *Rigoletto* so that the music flowed continuously, rather than being broken up into pieces. His music also matched the story more closely than had been usual before.

Rigoletto was different in another way, too. Each character sings a contrasting type of music, so that they all stand out clearly from one another. At one point, for example, there are four characters all singing at the same time. Although all their parts belong to the same musical structure, each of them expresses different feelings. It is a triumph of theatre music.

A modern production of *Rigoletto*, which cleverly transfers the story into the world of American gangsters.

In the same year, 1851, Verdi and Giuseppina Strepponi moved into a new home, the Villa Sant' Agata, near Busseto. They wanted a peaceful life in the country, and Verdi grew very interested in gardening. He also kept a close eye on the farming of his **estate**. But their happiness was ruined by hurtful gossip. This came not only from local people they did not know, but from Verdi's parents and Antonio Barezzi, too.

All these people were furious that Verdi was living with a woman who was not his wife. There were also whispers about Giuseppina's past – she had had lovers and illegitimate children. The couple therefore decided to shut themselves off from Busseto and lead an entirely private life.

A modern production of *Il Trovatore*.
One of the main parts requires the
singer to reach powerful high notes.

Verdi around the time he wrote *Il
Trovatore* and *La Traviata*, operas with
different plots but musical similarities.

HIGH DRAMA

espite Verdi's problems with the people of
Busseto, he did manage to compose in peace
at Sant' Agata. Between 1852 and 1853, he
composed two works in very quick succession. They
contained some of the finest music he had ever written.
The first was *Il Trovatore*, a complicated story about
gypsies, vengeance, murder, and two men who are rivals
for the same woman's love. It is a tragedy, full of drama
and passion. Parts of the **plot** seem absurd today because
they are too far-fetched to be believable. But the public
in Verdi's day loved deadly, dramatic stories.

Il Trovatore was instantly welcomed as Verdi's best work
yet. He had a great gift for inventing tunes that were both
beautiful and easy for audiences to remember. They were
also tailored perfectly to fit the singing voice. The operas
from this period of Verdi's working life are packed full of
magnificent tunes, one after the other.

The people who missed the old days of traditional Italian opera did not enjoy Verdi's new works. They did not like his choice of heroes – a gypsy bandit in *Il Trovatore* and a hunchback jester in *Rigoletto*. They preferred the days when opera's heroes were chosen from ancient Greek legends or Bible stories. Verdi's next opera made them even more upset. The leading lady was a **courtesan**.

This opera was called *La Traviata*, and although it was not liked at first, it has since become Verdi's best-loved work. The story is about Violetta, a beautiful but frail young woman. She falls in love with a young man, Alfredo, but eventually dies of **consumption**. It is less grand than some of Verdi's earlier works, but it contains much greater feeling. The music perfectly expresses the depth of Violetta's suffering. Unfortunately, *La Traviata*'s first performance was ruined by poor singing. The singer who played Violetta was also rather too plump to be convincing as a woman dying of consumption!

Teresa Stratas and Placido Domingo as Violetta and Alfredo in a 1983 film of Verdi's *La Traviata*.

A cartoon of Verdi taking part in the rehearsals of one of his operas. The singers wait quietly while the composer makes his wishes very plain.

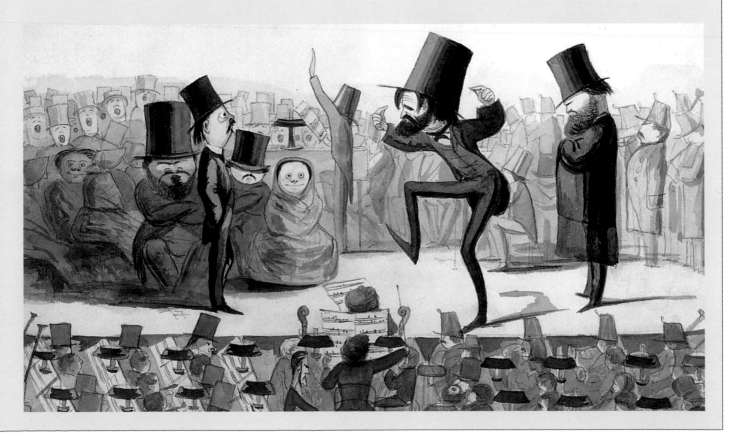

VIVA VERDI!

While Verdi was away from the Villa Sant' Agata, putting on his operas, Giuseppina had to stay at home in order to avoid any more scandal. But she sent Verdi long letters full of love and support. Eventually the couple decided that it would be better for everyone if they got married. So in August 1859, they travelled to the distant province of Savoy and had a secret wedding. Verdi could sometimes be a difficult and stubborn man, but their marriage was a long and happy one.

During the 1850s there was more unrest in Italy, as a new struggle against Austria began. Several other European countries now supported the idea of a free Italy, ruled by the King of Piedmont, Vittorio Emanuele.

It was at this time that Verdi, who was already well-known for his patriotism, became an important symbol of the freedom movement. The letters of his name were significant because they happened to spell out the first letters of a popular slogan of the time: **V**ittorio **E**manuele **R**e **D'I**talia (Vittorio Emanuele King of Italy). 'Viva VERDI!' ('Long live VERDI!') was shouted in the streets and painted on walls all over the country.

The Austrian emperor began to worry that he might lose control of Italy, and so made sure that his troops stationed there were ready for action. In April 1859, a war between Austria and Piedmont began. France joined in on the side of Piedmont. Two years later, on 17 March 1861, Italy was officially declared a united country with its own king, Vittorio Emanuele.

A wall-painting showing Italy's new king, Vittorio Emanuele (on the white horse), meeting the military leader Garibaldi.

CAVOUR (1810–1861)
AND GARIBALDI (1807–1882)

Camillo Cavour (left) spent much of his life in the service of the royal family of Piedmont. He was one of the leaders of the Risorgimento, and became Italy's first prime minister. His great skill was the ability to negotiate with leaders like Napoleon III of France. Cavour organized international alliances to support the new Italy. Tragically, he died shortly after his country was liberated. Verdi believed that Cavour was Italy's greatest hero.

Giuseppe Garibaldi (right) played a different but just as important part in the liberation of Italy. He began his career as a ship's captain, but later became a **guerrilla**. His adventures were famous worldwide. He became a national hero in Italy after he fought bravely against the Austrians in 1848. Then, in 1860, he led his men south and captured Naples and Sicily for Italy. Without Garibaldi, Italy might have remained divided in half.

This great victory was largely achieved by two remarkable leaders, a statesman called Camillo Cavour, and a courageous soldier called Giuseppe Garibaldi.

Cavour asked Verdi to be a **parliamentary candidate**, and he agreed. He served as a **deputy** until 1865, but rarely attended parliament, as he was busy composing.

Verdi on a visit to Russia, around 1861. He can be seen seated at the front of the sleigh, wrapped in a fur coat.

A MORE AMBITIOUS PROJECT

erdi now wanted to give up composing and retire to Sant' Agata. He still loved music, but disliked dealing with publishers, opera company managers and singers. In 1860 he decided to dedicate his life to gardening, farming and the countryside. His piano at Sant' Agata was left unopened, and guests were asked not to talk about music.

But Verdi was far from finished. In 1861 he was invited to write an opera for St Petersburg, in Russia. He travelled there to oversee the work, and was astonished at the harshness of the Russian winter. Then he retired to Sant' Agata once more.

It was not until 1866 that Verdi was persuaded to compose again. This time it was a large-scale opera for Paris. But as soon as he concentrated on composing, the old throat illness returned. There were other problems, too. Italy was preparing to go to war with Austria, and troops had gathered in the area around Busseto.

The opening ceremony of the Great Exhibition held in Paris in 1867. Verdi was one of its many visitors.

Verdi and Giuseppina realized that fighting would soon begin, so left for Paris in July 1866. This time they kept closely in touch with people at Sant' Agata, because they were concerned to have news about a little girl called Filomena. She was the daughter of one of Verdi's poor cousins, and in 1867 the composer adopted her as his own child.

Verdi's new opera, *Don Carlos*, was composed to fit in with musical taste in Paris. It was very long, covered a huge range of moods, and included spectacular scenery. The orchestral sound was also fuller and more expressive. Each character was vividly described in the music. For example, one of the most frightening characters, the Grand **Inquisitor**, was always introduced by a sinister, growling bass tune. It was immediately clear to the audience that a wicked, snake-like person had arrived on stage to take part in the action.

Verdi had become more ambitious. The first performance of *Don Carlos* took place in Paris on 11 March 1867 and marked a new stage in his development as a composer.

A cartoon of Verdi playing tunes from *Don Carlos* on a barrel organ.

THE SEVEN WEEKS' WAR

The Battle of Lissa cut Italy's rejoicing short just five years after freedom was won.

In June 1866 war broke out between the two great German-speaking nations, **Prussia** and Austria. They were rivals for power in northern Europe. Austria at this time still ruled the Italian province of Venice. Italy was therefore persuaded to join in the war against Austria, on the understanding that Venice would be made part of Italy as soon as a victory had been won.

Austria was swiftly defeated, and the conflict was called the Seven Weeks' War. All the important victories were won by Prussia. Italy suffered disastrous defeats, first at Custoza, and then at sea in the Battle of Lissa (right). This was one of the first sea-battles in which iron-plated battleships were used. But although the ships looked modern, the most important strategy used was an ancient one – ramming the enemy.

Verdi felt disappointed and humiliated by Italy's defeats. Nevertheless, after the Treaty of Vienna in October 1866, Venice was made part of Italy once more, as the Prussians had promised.

TRIUMPH IN EGYPT

Ismail Pasha, the Khedive of Egypt, was educated in Paris, and spent huge sums trying to make Egypt more European.

Verdi was a bit of a tyrant at home. He shouted at servants and farmers at Sant' Agata when they made mistakes, and when he received bad news, became depressed and short-tempered. Giuseppina coped with his moods as well as she could, but 1867 was a bad year. Within a few months, Verdi lost both men he called father – his real father, Carlo, and his **patron** Antonio Barezzi.

In 1869, the Suez Canal was opened in Egypt. The **Khedive** of Egypt built a new opera house in **Cairo** to celebrate the event. His greatest wish was for Verdi to write a work for the opening season. At first Verdi declined, but in the summer of 1870 began composing a grand opera on an ancient Egyptian subject, called *Aida*.

THE SUEZ CANAL

The Suez Canal is a manmade waterway in Egypt that separates the north-east tip of Africa from the mainland of Asia. It runs between the **Mediterranean Sea** in the north and the **Red Sea** in the south. Before the Suez Canal was built, European ships had to sail all the way around the southern tip of Africa in order to reach eastern countries, such as India and China. This was very time-consuming.

As far back as 1798, the French ruler Napoleon had planned to build a canal in Egypt, but the project was delayed until 1859. Work then began under the direction of a Frenchman, Ferdinand Lesseps, and continued for ten years. At first, local Egyptian peasants dug out the sand by hand and transported it away on camels. Later, steam-powered **dredgers** were used, and work progressed more quickly. The canal was eventually opened with much celebration in November 1869.

A procession of boats, carrying distinguished and royal visitors, passes through the Suez Canal at its opening ceremony on 17 November 1869.

The plot of the opera concerns an Egyptian general who is in love with his enemy's daughter, Aida. She is torn between loyalty to her father and her lover. The tale ends in tragedy, with the two lovers sealed inside a tomb chamber. The story was the work of a famous **Egyptologist** called Auguste Mariette. He also gave expert advice about ancient Egyptian customs and costumes for the production.

Aida was Verdi's last and most popular opera written in the grand French style. But it ran into difficulties even before it had been staged in Cairo for the first time.

Aida makes use of huge choruses and scenery. Here the cast are standing on a model of an Egyptian sphinx.

The first performance of *Aida* had to be postponed for a year, after the outbreak of war between Prussia and France in 1870. Paris, where all the costumes and scenery were stored, was besieged by Prussian troops for three months. Nothing could come in or go out of the city, and butchers were forced to sell cats, rats and dogs to their customers for food.

Aida was finally performed in Cairo on 24 December 1871, and was a great triumph. It is popular to this day for its grand music and spectacular staging.

A GLORIOUS COMEBACK

Alessandro Manzoni, one of Italy's greatest writers, died in 1873. Verdi, who admired him enormously, decided to write a **Requiem** in his memory. It was composed on a large scale, for soloists, chorus and orchestra. Parts of the Requiem sounded more like grand opera than church music. This is not surprising, as Verdi had spent a lifetime composing works designed for the theatre.

After the Requiem, Verdi sank into a depression and remained in a dark mood for several years. His old friends were dying and he was disappointed with politics in Italy. Everyone now assumed that he had retired for ever. They looked for a successor to carry on writing opera where the great Verdi had left off.

In 1879, Verdi's publisher, Giulio Ricordi, came up with an idea. He arranged for a well-known poet and composer called Arrigo Boito to prepare a libretto of Shakespeare's play *Othello*. He then asked Verdi if he would consider composing music for it. Verdi was interested, but promised nothing. Then, as the years passed, Verdi began to exchange more ideas with Boito, and the two men developed a good working relationship.

A caricature of Verdi conducting in 1879. It was published in the London magazine *Vanity Fair*, which always featured portraits of famous men.

VERDI AND WAGNER

The other outstanding opera composer of the nineteenth century was a German, Richard Wagner (1813–1883, right). He was born in the same year as Verdi, but the two men never met. They wrote completely different styles of opera, and the world saw them as rivals. Wagner created a new type of opera, in which there were no pauses for applause or vocal showpieces, as there were in Italian opera. Wagner also gave more importance to the orchestra. Parts of his operas sound like grand **symphonies**.

Wagner was a man of strong feelings, and he despised Italian opera, which he thought was shallow. He was extremely intelligent, and wrote all the words of his own operas. His greatest work was a four-opera cycle, called the *Ring of the Nibelungs*. Some people in Italy accused Verdi of being influenced by Wagner, especially in the later part of his career, when his operas became longer and his orchestral writing became heavier. Verdi hotly denied this. He had hardly ever heard Wagner's music. But Wagner's influence was so strong that his new style could not help filtering through to Italy.

In March 1884, at the age of 70, Verdi began to compose once more. But he was still reluctant, and did not complete his new work until December 1886. By this time all Italy was holding its breath. The great master had produced another opera after a gap of 15 years.

Boito's libretto for *Otello* (as it is spelt in Italian) was superb, and inspired Verdi to compose his greatest music yet. The story is about a general who wrongly believes that his wife has betrayed him. Everything Verdi had learnt about matching music to drama was perfected in *Otello*. All the characters, their thoughts and feelings, were clearly described in music.

Otello's première, on 5 February 1887, in Milan, was an historic event. The opera was hailed as Verdi's masterpiece, and crowds filled the streets shouting 'Viva Verdi!' all the way through the night.

Verdi (on the right) with Arrigo Boito at the Villa Sant' Agata. The two men respected each other enormously.

Singer Placido Domingo as Otello in a film version of Verdi's great opera.

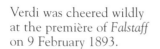

Verdi was cheered wildly at the première of *Falstaff* on 9 February 1893.

FALSTAFF

Despite Verdi's age, he still had a spark of adventure in him. It was not long before Boito persuaded him to start another opera. This time the story was drawn from four different Shakespeare plays, which all feature a fat, funny character called Sir John Falstaff.

Verdi (with the umbrella) visiting the site of his musicians' retirement home. The architect stands next to him.

Verdi's opera *Falstaff* was his first comedy for over 50 years. He enjoyed composing it, and the result was sensational. His skill as a composer and his understanding of drama had increased with age. *Falstaff* is described by many as his greatest and most revolutionary work. Verdi conducted the première himself, aged 80, at La Scala in Milan. *Falstaff* and *Otello* were then staged at every major opera house in the world. Verdi had reached the peak of his career.

BRAINSE CABRACH
CABRA BRANCH
TEL: 8691414

In 1895 Verdi began a project that was very important to him. He wanted to build a retirement home in Milan to house 100 poor and elderly musicians, and became closely involved with the design and building work. It was one of the many charitable causes to which the composer contributed generous sums of money.

Verdi as an old man still kept an interest in politics, and continued to have great influence over the world of Italian music.

Meanwhile Verdi continued to compose. 'I am destined to work until my last gasp,' he wrote. But his final works were not operatic, they were religious. They are known as his *Four Sacred Pieces*. One of them in particular, the **Te Deum**, contains some of his most beautiful music.

On 14 November 1897, Giuseppina died with Verdi at her side. The old composer was devastated. But he struggled on and continued to see his many friends, either in Milan or at the Villa Sant' Agata.

Then, on 21 January 1901, Verdi had a **stroke** as he was dressing in his Milan hotel room. Just six days later he died, surrounded by friends. All Italy went into mourning. Verdi had asked for no music to be played at his funeral. But the vast crowd that followed his coffin through the streets began softly to sing his famous chorus from *Nabucco*, 'Va, pensiero'.

Verdi's funeral procession. He was buried side by side with his wife in the musicians' retirement home he had founded.

1813   Giuseppe Verdi born at Le Roncole, Italy, 9 October.

1823   Becomes organist at Le Roncole.

1832   Travels to Milan, but fails entrance exam at conservatory.

1836   Marries Margherita Barezzi, 4 May.
Becomes music director in Busseto.

1839   Leaves Busseto and settles in Milan.
Première of *Oberto*, Milan, 17 November.

1840   Margherita dies, 18 June.

1842   Première of *Nabucco*, Milan, 9 March.

1847   Première of *Macbeth*, Florence, 14 March.
Begins life with Giuseppina Strepponi.

1848   Revolution in France, February. Louis-Philippe abdicates.
'Five Days' revolt in Milan, March.
Buys estate at Sant' Agata, near Busseto, May.

1851   Première of *Rigoletto*, Venice, 11 March.
Moves to Sant' Agata with Giuseppina.

1853   Première of *Il Trovatore*, Rome, 19 January.
Première of *La Traviata*, Venice, 6 March.

1859   War between Piedmont and Austria begins, April.
Marries Giuseppina in Savoy, 29 August.

1861   Elected to parliament, January.
Italy officially declared a united country, 17 March.

1866   Seven Weeks' War breaks out between Austria, Prussia
and Italy, June.

1867   Death of Carlo Verdi, 14 January.
Première of *Don Carlos*, Paris, 11 March.
Death of Antonio Barezzi, 21 July.
Adopts seven-year-old Filomena Verdi.

1869   Opening of Suez Canal, 17 November.

1871   Première of *Aida*, Cairo, 24 December.

1874   Conducts first performance of Requiem, in memory of
Alessandro Manzoni, Milan, 22 May.

1879   Idea for *Otello* first discussed with Ricordi and Boito.

1887   Première of *Otello*, Milan, 5 February.

1893   Conducts première of *Falstaff*, Milan, 9 February.

1895   Begins work on musicians' retirement home, Milan.

1897   Death of Giuseppina, 14 November.

1901   Giuseppe Verdi dies in Milan, 27 January.

abdicate to resign from a position of power or leadership.

amateur somebody who is not professional. Amateurs can be very skilled, but they use their skills for enjoyment rather than to make money.

aria a song for a solo singer. 'aria' is the Italian for 'air', which is also a musical term for 'tune'.

Babylon an ancient city in the Middle East, and the centre of an empire. Babylon's greatest period was 1800–500 BC.

barrel organ a large music box that sounds like an organ and plays tunes when its handle is turned. In nineteenth-century Italy, barrel organs were a popular form of street entertainment, like busking.

Cairo the capital city of Egypt.

censor a government officer whose job is to check everything that is published or performed, to make sure nothing offensive is included. In some countries, censors seriously restrict the freedom of artists, writers and musicians.

commission to invite a composer to write a piece of music for an agreed price.

conservatory a word used to describe a music college.

consumption a serious infection that attacks the lungs. Before a cure was found, consumption often killed the people who suffered from it. The modern name for this disease is tuberculosis.

courtesan an attractive woman who is paid to escort and entertain gentlemen.

Crusader one of the medieval Christian soldiers who set out from Europe to fight wars, called Crusades, in the Holy Land. Crusaders carried banners showing the Christian cross.

curtain-call the moment at the end of a performance in the theatre when the performers line up on stage to receive applause. If an audience in nineteenth-century Italy did not like a performance, the curtain-call was the time when they booed, hissed and sometimes threw things at the performers.

deputy somebody who is appointed to do a job on behalf of other people, such as (in this example) a member of parliament.

dredger a boat designed to scoop mud from the bottom of a river.

Duchy a state or province that is ruled by a duke.

Egyptologist a historian whose special interest is ancient Egypt.

estate a large area of property, which may include farms and parkland, often attached to the owner's main house.

exile when people live in a foreign country and cannot return to their homeland, they are described as 'in exile'. They are also called exiles.

galley a wooden ship, like those used in Roman times, that requires a team of rowers to make it go forward in the water. Galley slaves were often foreign prisoners of war, and lived in harsh conditions.

guerrilla a soldier who fights wars like a bandit, and is not in the pay of an official government.

Inquisitor a member of the Roman Catholic Church whose job was to interrogate people suspected of being enemies of the Church. Inquisitors were strict and sometimes ruthless in the punishments they enforced.

Khedive the title given to the ruler of Egypt between 1867 and 1914, the years when the country was ruled by the Turkish empire.

libretto the book or words of an opera. The people who write librettos are called librettists.

Mediterranean Sea the sea in southern Europe that is almost completely enclosed by land. It divides Europe from Africa, and stretches between Spain in the west and Turkey in the east.

nationalist a person who strongly supports his or her own country and culture.

opera a musical drama in which the performers sing most or all of their lines. The music in an opera is just as important as the words.

parliamentary candidate somebody who is chosen to compete for election to parliament.

Parma a province and city in the north of Italy.

patriot somebody who is proud and supportive of his or her country.

patron a person who supports an artist by providing money or employment.

Piedmont a region in north-west Italy that borders France and Switzerland. The capital is Turin.

plot the story of an opera, a play or a book.

première the first performance of a new work.

Prussia a powerful state in north-east Germany. When Germany became a single country, in 1871, the Prussian royal family ruled as emperors.

recitative a piece of speech set to music, in which the words are more important than the tune. A recitative usually introduces an aria, and helps to move the story forward quickly.

Red Sea a sea to the north-east of Africa, separating Africa from Asia. It stretches from the Mediterranean Sea in the north to the Indian Ocean in the south.

republican a person who supports a system of government that does not include monarchs or emperors. A republican believes rulers should be elected by all the people.

Requiem a Christian church ceremony usually performed at funerals.

Saracen a word used to describe muslims who fought against the Crusaders in the Holy Land during the Middle Ages.

Shakespeare, William (1564–1616) English poet and playwright, admired across the world as one of the greatest writers who ever lived.

spinet a type of small keyboard instrument, popular from the late seventeenth century through to the end of the eighteenth century.

stroke a sudden illness caused by a blood clot in the brain. Some strokes are mild, and patients recover. Others leave people paralysed, or even cause death.

symphony a large-scale piece of music written for orchestra. Symphonies are usually divided into three or four sections, called movements, which contrast with one another.

Te Deum a Christian prayer of worship, written in Latin, and often set to music by composers. Translated into English, it begins with the words, 'We praise thee, O God, we acknowledge thee to be the Lord.'

INDEX

BRAINSE CABRACH
CABRA BRANCH
TEL: 8691414